Burn The BLUEPRINT

A JOURNEY FROM HUSTLE TO HEALING

MAGAN AVILA

Burn the Blueprint Copyright © 2025 by Magan Avila.

All rights reserved. No part of this publication may be reproduced, distributed or transmitted in any form or by any means, including photocopying, recording, or other electronic or mechanical methods, without the prior written permission of the publisher, except in the case of brief quotations embodied in critical reviews and certain other noncommercial uses permitted by copyright law.

Although the author and publisher have made every effort to ensure that the information in this book was correct at press time, the author and publisher do not assume and hereby disclaim any liability to any party for any loss, damage, or disruption caused by errors or omissions, whether such errors or omissions result from negligence, accident, or any other cause.

Disclaimer: This book is designed to provide general information for our readers. It is sold with the understanding that the publisher is not engaged to render any type of legal, business or any other kind of professional advice. The content of this book is the sole expression and opinion of the author, and not necessarily that of the publisher. No warranties or guarantees are expressed or implied by the author's choice to include any of the content in this book. Neither the publisher nor the author shall be liable for any physical, psychological, emotional, financial, or commercial damages, including, but not limited to, special, incidental, consequential or other damages. The reader is responsible for their own choices, actions, and results.

Published by Prominence Publishing.

Burn the Blueprint / Avila, Magan. -- 1st ed.

ISBN: 978-1-997649-21-2

Table of Contents

Introduction 1

Who Am I, Really? 5

Burnout, The Breakdown Before The Breakthrough..... 15

The Peace You've Been Chasing 25

Becoming Her 31

Softness is Not Weakness 41

Burning the Blueprint 49

The Rise of the Real You 59

Unlearning the Lies 71

Trusting Yourself Again (Even When the Old You Shows Up) 83

Where She Begins 91

About the Author 97

Introduction

To anyone who procrastinated, delayed, made excuses, or straight-up quit, I'm writing this for you. The "I'm not worthy" or "who am I?" thoughts can be overwhelming, loud, and all-consuming, but there is a truth that you may need to hear just as much as I did.

As I write this, I am not proud to say that it has taken me five years just to get these words down on paper. The voices in my head have been running the show called my life for many years, but today, *today*, I am taking back control. Even if only for the ten minutes I currently have before my son realizes I've left the room. Imposter syndrome is a real thing, and my goodness, does it just love to take control. Maybe it's just me, but I have found that if I don't actively keep my thoughts in check, fear and doubt take over like a tornado in a trailer park.

The truth is that life does not have to be this hard. It's hard enough juggling everything on our to-do lists. Whether you have kids, a business, a husband, or all the above, life has its own challenges that it will always throw at you. Why do we allow these lies to take control and make everything that much harder? Maybe because we don't know any better. Maybe we don't know how to make them stop. Or even worse, maybe we don't believe, deep down, that we are worthy of something better. Whatever your reason is, I hope this finds you in a place where you're open to hearing the truth. Truly hearing the truth is almost just as hard, though.

Accepting something different than what you have built your life on can seem daunting and impossible. But I'm here to tell you, encourage you, that there is another way. A better way! The truth is that you are worthy! You are qualified! Someone out there needs what you have to offer. It does not matter what that thing is; I promise someone else needs it. Someone, somewhere, is struggling like you are, or like you were. If you can help even just one person in the great big world not suffer quite as much as you did, isn't that enough validation that you are qualified?

This realization for me was transformational. I don't have all the answers, and never will. But what I do have is experience, past and present. Am I a hypocrite for writing these words while I'm still struggling with them myself? Maybe some will think so. But I believe they will also help someone as well, even if that someone is me. At the end of the day, I just want to do my best. Make a difference in this circus of a life I get to call mine. Even in the days when this 'circus' is a shit-show, I can take some comfort in knowing that at least I'm the ring leader. I get to choose what I do when I wake up: coffee or water, meditation or TV, playing with my kids or doom-scrolling. I get to choose.

I can't control the massive storm outside that's currently screwing with my internet and making my 5-year-old complain, but I can control how I respond to the chaos. To me, when I stop and think about that for a minute, it's kind of beautiful. Imagine if we truly had control over everything...OH SHIT! What if everything from the weather to the traffic was up to us? Every day. No, thank you! I struggle with making the right decisions, given the limited control I currently have, much less over everything else.

We like to believe that if we could just control everything, we would be better off. But let's face It, would we really? Are we truly the most qualified to make all the right decisions all the time? About all the things? I would love to think that I am, but my life proves that I'm not, and something tells me you're not either.

So, do we want more control, OR do we want more intention with what we do have control over? This is a question I often ask myself. Accepting things that I cannot control is usually downright scary. Whether you believe in a higher power or not, there's something or someone that is controlling things we cannot. We can choose to make peace with that, and that's the dirt right there. The

INTRODUCTION

very beginning of change. The catalyst to the next step in your own circus.

So, back to the question of "who am I?". Well, only you can truly answer that, but I can most definitely tell you who you are not. You are not the product of failures or mistakes. You are not the product of missteps and letdowns. Those have made you into who you are today, but they are not who you are. You are who you choose to be! Let me say that again for those who need it to sink in deep: YOU ARE WHO YOU CHOOSE TO BE! That means who you are can change.

Actually, who you are will change. Just as you are not the same person you were when you were five, you will not be the same twenty years from now. Life happens in between. But the one thing that will remain constant no matter how much time or life passes is that you will always be worthy! Worthy of success. Worthy of joy. Worthy of peace. Worthy of love. Worthy of happiness. I could go on and on, but you get what I'm saying.

Your worth will never change, even when you do. And that, my friend, is the foundation on which your mindset needs to stand. You can have a Master's in every subject or a GED; your worth is still the same. You can have a laundry list of 'failures' or a thousand Fortune 500 companies; your worth is still the same. If you take nothing else from me, or stop reading right now, I hope that you at least take this truth with you.

CHAPTER 1

Who Am I, Really?

Burning the candle at both ends. We've all heard the saying, and honestly, most of us have probably done it at least once or twice. As I'm writing this, I find myself in a season of constantly burning the candle at both ends, to the point that my candle is just about melted. Despite the negative thoughts (lies) that are creeping into my head as we speak, I am going to share with you what I have learned, and I am still practicing. Burning that candle constantly only leads to burnout. And I promise, once you're in burnout mode, it is hell trying to claw your way out of it. But, fortunately, it's not impossible—some excellent news for those of you who may be in burnout right now. However, I want to focus on how to prevent us from getting there in the first place before sharing how I've learned to escape the burnout cycle.

First, let's define burnout, shall we? Burnout is a form of exhaustion caused by being in a constant state of chaos, or emotional, physical, or mental fatigue. This is how I define it, anyway. There are multiple definitions on Google if this one doesn't tickle your fancy. It's just as important to know what burnout means as it is to recognize and understand its signs and symptoms. The most common signs I have noticed are brain fog, constant feeling of exhaustion, mood swings, forgetfulness, insomnia or sleeping too much, and depressive episodes. While these may not all apply to you, I'm willing to bet that you have experienced at least one of these symptoms within the past year, six months, hell, or maybe even six days, like me. Now that we can pinpoint the signs, you are the one who has to decide if you're in burnout or on your way to it. Unfortunately, I can't decide that for you. But if you do find yourself there, I can help you avoid a total breakdown. This may seem like a "do as I say, not as I do" moment coming from me, to those that know me well, but it is something you will have to work on A LOT. Sometimes daily. But, oh, is it worth it! There will be harder days than others, but in the end, finding a balance and living in alignment will be more than worth the tears and hard work. I PROMISE!

Now, let's get down to it. How do you avoid a complete meltdown from burnout? First, let's start with your mental state. I need you to get this concept ingrained in your mind: rest is not earned, it's required! I can tell you so many personal stories where I failed to believe this and ended up unable to get out of bed, on medication, and even being hospitalized. Reaching this point is definitely not where you want to be. If you believe, deep down, that you have to work hard enough to earn or deserve a break, GIRL, STOP IT! That is nothing but a huge LIE that you need to shut down right now before your body shuts down for you. The whole "I'll sleep when I'm dead" concept needs to burn in hell.

I know that as women, moms, multipreneurs, wives, and so much more, we seem to have been raised with the notion that focusing on ourselves is a bad thing, even selfish. But if resting to avoid shutting down is considered selfish to others, then fuck them and you do you boo! Yes, I just dropped the f-bomb, I am that serious and need you to hear me! Rest is your best friend. I'm not talking about being lazy; there's a difference. Rest is necessary for our brains and bodies to function correctly. I'm also not just talking about getting a good night's sleep, although that's important too. Rest can be something as simple as stepping away from your computer and standing outside for five minutes, taking a shower (preferably without kids), going for a quick drive, reading a chapter of your favorite book, or my favorite, 10 minutes of silence while drinking a fresh cup of coffee that hasn't been re-warmed in the microwave at least 3 times.

Rest is giving your brain and body a break from the task or tasks you're currently doing. Sitting down at the computer for hours to get work done is often said to be one of the most effective ways to be productive, but what if I told you that taking a twenty-minute break after sitting for that time is more productive? Twenty to thirty minutes of pure focus is excellent, but then give your brain a rest. Believe me, I understand pressure and deadlines. My to-do list would likely make your head spin, but stick with me here for a minute. Giving your brain a break allows it to recover and become more efficient, as well as more creative. Now, how long the break is up to you, but I would recommend at least ten minutes. Don't get carried away and spend hours doom-scrolling, then try to go back to work. What you do during that rest or break is just as important, if not more important, as how long you take. This is where you want to find your balance, likely through trial and error. For me, thirty minutes of working and ten minutes of just sitting outside or listening to my favorite playlist work wonders. It took me about two weeks of experimenting daily to find what works best for me, but it's different for everyone. The important thing is to see what works best for you and stick to it religiously. Shut off all distractions: kids, phone, emails, social media, everything. Then, when that timer goes off, GET UP! Step away from what you're doing. Change rooms if possible. Get away! Set a timer for your break, then get back to work. This may seem challenging at first, but the results you achieve will make it all worthwhile.

My second hack for avoiding burnout is much more challenging, but it is much more rewarding. It's setting boundaries and non-negotiables. This part gets deep and requires a lot more practice and self-compassion. I want to start by first saying that we are working towards progress, not perfection, here. Boundaries are so vital to progress in anything you're doing. This can be saying 'no', eliminating habits that aren't serving you, stepping back from relationships that aren't helping you grow, and maybe even letting go of people you care about. This is the hardest part, but it is just as necessary. We all have the same amount of time in any given day, twenty-four hours. This is not news; we are all aware of this. We can't control everything that happens within that period, but we can control whether we're setting ourselves up for success or failure. Overscheduling ourselves does not serve us. Those bad habits that bring you momentary satisfaction but leave you feeling *ick* don't serve you. People that constantly drain your time, energy, and joy don't serve you. If you don't respect your time, how can you expect anyone else to?

Every day, you need to have non-negotiables and standards by which you make decisions. Before saying 'yes' to something that someone is asking of you, first ask yourself these questions:

1) *What will I be giving up in order to do this?* There is always something that must be sacrificed when you take on something new. This could be time, energy, sleep, or many other things.

2) *Do I currently have the energy and time to give this the attention that it deserves?* You don't want to do anything half-assed, right? Therefore, you need to ask yourself if you have the means to give this the time, energy, and focus it deserves. This is where you will find yourself answering 'no' the most.

3) *Am I the most qualified person to do this thing?* Sometimes saying 'no' can be you giving the name of someone else who would be better equipped to do what this person is asking of you. You have resources, girl, utilize them! If editing someone's paper, running a meeting, helping out with teacher lunches, or whatever it may be, is not something you're particularly good at, do you know someone else who is?

Now that we have briefly discussed boundaries, let's talk about non-negotiables and personal commitment. This isn't the sexiest of things to talk about, but if you want to grow, it is required. I believe that everyone should have daily non-negotiables. These are things that you will do every single day, no matter what life decides to throw at you. Activities such as showering, participating in spiritual devotionals, praying, meditating, drinking a certain amount of water, waking up at a specific time, going to bed at a designated time, reading a bedtime story to children, and so on. No matter what happens, there are things that you must commit to doing *no matter what.*

Choosing what these things are is much simpler than you might think. Just off the top of your head, what are three things you can do every day that your future self will thank you for? These are your daily non-negotiables. I have different ones for each area of my life: personal, spiritual, and relational. Every day, I will drink water, do my spiritual devotional, and wake up by 9 am, NO MATTER WHAT! This is what works for me and my schedule in my current season. I work late, so it doesn't make sense for me to decide to wake up at 6 am, but for others, that may be a sensible choice. For someone who works a 9-to-5 job, waking up earlier may be a non-negotiable. Whatever your current season looks like, you need to pick your non-negotiables and STICK TO THEM FOR DEAR LIFE! Watch the transformation that happens! This is where personal commitment comes into play. It's not enough to say or vow to do these things every day. You need to promise yourself. That means, before you hit that pillow, you make sure you have completed all your non-negotiables for the day. There's more to it than growth, though; each time you make a promise to yourself and you keep it, you're building trust within yourself. What happens when you build trust within yourself? Transformation is unlocked! Your confidence increases! You are strengthened! You can't expect to be able to keep a promise to others if you can't keep the ones you make for yourself.

It's all about building a strong foundation. Taking the time to rest, setting boundaries, and committing to daily non-negotiables are the most significant steps you can take to prevent burnout. While I know firsthand how hard this is, I also understand how unbearably difficult it is to live life in a state of burnout. If you are one of the unfortunate ones experiencing full-blown burnout right now, I want to say that my heart goes out to you. Burnout is an extremely exhausting state to be in. However, I also want to say that I know how to help you! It takes time, but it is possible to get through to the other side. The better side. The healthier side. The peaceful side. Much like avoiding burnout, rest is also an important factor in recovering from it. You must make time to rest, as we have already discussed how important it is. However, if you're in burnout, rest is the most crucial component in helping you recover.

Secondly, ask for help—just one thing, just one person, even if it's just one thing. Just ask! Are you the only one who can pick up your kids from school? Are you the only one who can load the dishwasher? Are you the only one who can decide what is for dinner? I'm willing to bet there's someone out there who can take at least one of these off your plate for you. Asking for help is a strong lesson in learning to let go of control. It may not be done how you would do it, but it gets done. And right now, that needs to be enough. The concept of 'enough' will be your best friend right now. Not forever, but at least for right now. Having cereal for dinner is enough. Pacifying your kids with a tablet today is enough. Doing the bare minimum right now is enough.

Give yourself grace during this time and be gentle with yourself. Take extra time for things that bring you joy. Take the time to watch the episode you haven't had time to sit down for. Take that bubble bath and light those candles. Hell, even splurge and take that nap your body has been craving. Listen to your body and mind, give them what they need in this season. Remember, this is temporary, and it won't be like this forever as long as you take the time to work through it.

There are many things I could focus on to help you overcome burnout, but I want to make this as simple and easy to start as possible. These two steps—rest and ask for help (or delegate)— are the fastest and most impactful steps I have found that help. What I want you to understand is the importance of giving yourself grace during this period. Remember, we are looking for progress, not perfection! It doesn't happen overnight, but I'm willing to bet that if you practice these steps, within a week you will start to feel different. And once you feel different, you can use that as the catalyst for making significant changes. Work backwards through the steps I've given in this chapter. Once you've become accustomed to focusing on rest and asking for help, start working through the steps I mentioned that help prevent burnout, such as setting boundaries and non-negotiables. If you put in the work, you will see the reward. You're not alone, that I can promise you! If no one else can, know that I can relate and I am cheering you on. You can do this, and it will get better. Just focus on doing what you can, when you can, and listen to what your brain and body need.

CHAPTER 2

Burnout, The Breakdown Before The Breakthrough

Imagine wanting something so badly that the pain of not having it consumes your entire body. Maybe you can relate. I'm not talking about wanting a particular career, fame, money, or even love. I'm talking about peace. For years, I spun my wheels, thinking that if I just hustled hard enough, I would have the cushy life I wanted so badly. It wasn't until recently that I realized what I was chasing after was a life of alignment. I always knew something was missing, but I could never pinpoint what it was. I went to a women's conference in 2022, and while there, I gained so much insight that would eventually change my whole life. Living out of alignment can lead to so much chaos, unfulfillment, and restlessness. Living your life each day in alignment with your core values is the true path to fulfillment and peace. However, to achieve this, you must first identify your core values.

What are the top three things you value most? Is it your faith? Your family? Honesty? Integrity? Those things are your core values, and they are where your daily alignment starts. Being aligned means every decision you make is first screened through the filter of your core values. Before you make a choice or say 'yes' to something, you first make sure that it aligns with your values. Will what you're being asked to do require you to compromise on something? Will it take time away from what matters most? These are questions you should ask every day, likely multiple times a day. Earlier, I wrote about non-negotiables, and living a life of alignment begins with those non-negotiables.

For most of my life, I didn't ask those questions. I just said yes to everything and everyone, because I thought that's what good people do. One of my core values is serving others, so naturally, I thought I was doing the right thing. I believed that helping others meant sacrificing myself. I didn't realize that every "yes" that pulled me away from my values was actually a quiet "no" to the life I wanted.

Looking back, there were so many moments where I knew deep down something wasn't right, but I pushed through anyway, out of fear, obligation, or the belief that I just needed to try harder. I was exhausted. Burnt out. And still unfulfilled. It wasn't until I started identifying my core values—really naming them—that I began to see the misalignment everywhere. My calendar, my work, even my relationships. It was like trying to run a race in shoes that didn't fit. No matter how fast I moved, I always ended up in pain. But once I began making decisions from a place of alignment, everything shifted. I started saying no more. I prioritized rest without guilt. I stopped chasing what looked good on the outside and started choosing what felt right on the inside. And guess what? The peace I was chasing... it began to show up. Slowly, quietly, but undeniably.

But here's the thing no one tells you about alignment: it's not a one-time decision. It's a *daily* commitment. It's not glamorous or always clear. It often feels inconvenient. Sometimes, alignment looks like disappointing people. It looks like walking away from something that's "almost right" but not *quite*. It looks like turning down opportunities that don't fit, *even when you're desperate for a win*. And that's where it got really hard for me. Because I didn't want to let people down. I didn't want to seem ungrateful. And, if I'm honest, I was scared that if I didn't take every opportunity that came my way, I'd miss my one shot at building the life I wanted. But what I've learned—through trial, error, and a lot of internal wrestling—is that alignment *never* asks you to betray yourself. It never demands that you give up your peace for progress. And if something does? It's not meant for you. Not right now. Maybe not ever.

Alignment isn't about perfection. It's about intentionality. It's about getting honest enough to admit when something doesn't feel right, even if it makes sense on paper. It's about tuning in to that quiet voice inside that says, "This isn't who we are," and actually listening. Once I began being intentional with every action I made, alignment sort of just followed. I started with something tiny and simple—my social media posts. Instead of perfectly put together, Canva created graphics with a well-thought-out post to go along with it, usually with the help of Chat GPT, I started being more intentional and authentic with what I was posting. I started posting more pictures of myself, along with captions that truly reflected my thoughts or what I had learned that day. I started focusing more on helping someone instead of portraying a facade of "everything is alright, just hang in there." And honestly, it felt uncomfortable at first. Vulnerable. Exposed. I was so accustomed to presenting a polished version of myself, the kind of person I thought people wanted to see. But when I started showing up as the *real* me—the messy, growing, learning me—something shifted. People began responding not just with likes or comments, but with real messages. Real connection. They didn't need perfection. They needed honesty. And in showing up that way, I was healing a part of myself, too—the part that was tired of pretending, tired of hustling, tired of hiding behind a brand.

That's the thing about alignment: it creates clarity. It attracts the right people. It opens the right doors. But more importantly, it brings you back to *yourself*. Every little aligned decision, no matter how small, starts to build a life that feels like home. So if you're reading this and feeling the weight of misalignment, start small.

Ask yourself:

- Where am I performing instead of being?
- What am I saying yes to that doesn't match my values?
- What would it look like to live just 1% more aligned tomorrow?

Because peace doesn't come from finally arriving, it comes from choosing alignment in the little moments, over and over again. Alignment isn't about achieving perfection—it's about returning to the truth of who you are. It's about choosing intentionality over performance, peace over pressure, values over validation. I'm still learning this every day. I still wrestle with it. But I've lived out of alignment before, and I know the toll it takes. I care too much about my peace to go back there.

If something in you feels unsettled, disconnected, or "off"... you're not crazy. You might just be out of alignment. Start small. Pay attention. Ask yourself the hard questions. Trust that even the tiniest act of alignment is a step toward peace because peace doesn't come from doing more. It comes from becoming more of who you were always meant to be. I know that sounds counterintuitive, especially when life is loud and messy. But peace isn't the absence of chaos. It's the presence of clarity. It's a calm rooted so deeply in your values and self-trust that even when things around you are falling apart, something inside you holds steady. Have you ever known someone who remained completely calm amid chaos? Maybe they were facing grief, transition, uncertainty—and yet, they carried this quiet steadiness. That kind of peace is available to all of us. But it doesn't come from avoiding hard things. It comes from being anchored.

Anchored in truth.

Anchored in purpose.

Anchored in who you really are.

That's the power of alignment. It doesn't eliminate life's storms, but it gives you the deep-seated roots to withstand them.

My major reality check came out of nowhere and was not at all subtle. I didn't have a breakdown. There wasn't some dramatic moment or big crisis that forced me to stop. It was quieter than that. I just woke up one morning and realized I was depressed. Like, feel-it-in-my-bones, miserable. And not because anything was *wrong*. I had people I loved. A life that, on paper, looked fine. I mean, there were struggles, but nothing new or significant. But something inside me felt off—like I was floating through my days on autopilot. Just existing. I couldn't quite put my finger on it at first. It wasn't that I hated my work or my life. It's that none of it felt like *mine*. I was doing what I thought I was *supposed* to do. What other people had praised me for. What made sense. What seemed responsible. But somewhere along the way, I stopped asking what made me come alive. I stopped checking in with my soul. And when I finally got quiet enough to listen, I realized something heartbreaking: I was living for everyone else, but not for myself. I felt like I was running on a treadmill I never agreed to step on. Always moving, always giving, always hustling—but never getting anywhere. There was no destination—just distance. I had traded fulfillment for performance and purpose for approval. And I was tired. I wrestled hard with guilt. Because how could I feel this way when I had so much to be grateful for? How could I want *more* when others had less? But here's what I know now: gratitude doesn't mean settling. You can love the people in your life and still feel misaligned. You can be grateful for what you have and still long for something deeper. And I did. That was the day something in me shifted. I didn't have a plan yet. But I knew I couldn't keep living like that. I couldn't keep betraying myself for the sake of keeping everything "okay" on the outside. That was the beginning of my journey back to alignment. Not because someone told me I should, but because my soul finally got loud enough that I couldn't ignore it anymore. Maybe you've felt that too. That quiet ache. That feeling like you're doing everything "right," yet still carrying a sense of restlessness. Maybe you've built a life that looks good to everyone else but doesn't feel quite right to you. If any of that resonates, I want to gently ask you:

- When was the last time you checked in with yourself, not to assess your productivity, but your peace?
- Are you living in alignment with what matters most to you, or just running to keep up with expectations?
- What part of your life feels like a treadmill right now? What would it take to slow down and step off?

You don't need a dramatic wake-up call to start changing. You don't need a perfect plan. You just need honesty—and the courage to stop running long enough to listen. Peace doesn't come when everything outside of you gets easier. It comes when you stop abandoning yourself for the sake of what's expected. Alignment starts with one honest question at a time. You don't have to blow up your life to begin again. You don't need to have it all figured out. Sometimes the most powerful change starts with a whisper, not a shout. A whisper from your soul saying,

"There's more for you than this." Alignment isn't a destination you arrive at—it's a daily decision. And peace? It's not something you chase. It's something you create, one small, honest, intentional step at a time. You deserve to live a life that feels like yours. Not one designed by other people's expectations, but one built on your values, your truth, and your purpose. Even if it takes time. Even if it's scary, even if no one else understands it yet, because real peace isn't found in what you do for others, it's found in what you're finally willing to do for *yourself*. This is your permission to begin again. To listen deeper. To live more honestly. To choose alignment—even when it's hard. Because the life you're craving? The peace you've been chasing? It's already inside you. You're just finding your way back to it.

CHAPTER 3

The Peace You've Been Chasing

When I began stepping away from the constant hustle, I expected peace to rush in. What I didn't expect was the *emptiness*. Not because I missed the chaos, but because I didn't know who I was without it. For so long, I had tied my value to how much I could juggle. How much I could achieve. How much I could endure. Slowing down felt like failure. Rest felt like laziness. And the quiet made me question everything. Was I valuable if I wasn't producing something or helping someone? Oh, how my brain started a negative thought spiral. I learned the hard way what happens when you place your value in what you can do versus who you are. Once I slowed down and these thoughts started invading my mind, it became clear how much false comfort I had taken in the feeling of being needed, being busy, always helping, and never saying 'no', among other things. I say it's false comfort because, though it sometimes felt nice, like being needed, ultimately, all I was doing was keeping myself busy enough not to hear my wants. I was shocked when fear began to take over my emotions. Like, why? What was I so afraid of? I was genuinely confused. But after forcing myself to be still, quiet, and listen to that small voice inside, it all came to light. It was so easy for me to get caught up in the chaos and busyness because it was the perfect distraction. As long as I was busy and doing 'good' things to boot, I didn't have to focus on me. On the pain, insecurity, fear, doubt, hopelessness, none of it. I just didn't have time.

I have known many people in my life who struggle with addiction, in some way, shape, or form. But I never thought I was one of them. It turns out that busyness can be used as a way to escape your problems the same way people can use drugs, alcohol, sex, you name it, to escape their problems. This was truly earth-shattering for me. My hustle kept me busy enough that I never stopped to ask myself if I was actually okay. And man, was I a mess. When you live out of alignment for so long, it can seem impossible to get back in it, but I was determined more than I had ever been for anything.

I realized my first step was learning how to be okay with just being. Seems pretty simple, doesn't it? Just sit somewhere in silence for two minutes. No phone. No to-do list. No background noise. Just you, your breath, your thoughts. But little did I know that small step would be one of the hardest I'd ever taken. It took me weeks—maybe even months—to sit still without unraveling. I'd try to quiet my mind, but my thoughts would race: *Did I forget something? Should I be doing something else? Why is this so uncomfortable?* I couldn't stop bouncing my leg. My breathing would grow shallow. Some days I'd cry—not because of what was happening in the silence, but because of what I could *finally hear* without the distractions. And honestly? I hated it at first. Because for the first time in a long time, I had to face myself without a filter.

No busyness to hide behind. No productivity to prove my worth. Just... me. It felt like being exposed. Like holding up a mirror to all the parts of myself I had pushed aside in favor of hustle. The doubt. The fear. The ache of unworthiness I didn't even know was still there. But I stayed with it even when it felt pointless. Even when I wanted to run. Because something in me knew—*if I couldn't be okay with stillness, I'd never be truly at peace.* Slowly, the silence started to feel less like a threat and more like an invitation. An invitation to come home to myself. To release the pressure. To breathe deeper. To stop performing. And in those tiny, quiet moments—when I stopped trying to fix, earn, or prove—I started to feel something I hadn't felt in a long time: *Enough.* Just me. Just being. And that was the beginning of everything.

If you're anything like I was, the idea of slowing down might sound impossible—or even a little terrifying. Maybe stillness feels unsafe because it's in the quiet that everything you've been avoiding finally catches up. Maybe it's where doubt lives. Or grief. Or truth. But here's what I want you to know:

- You're not weak because rest feels hard
- You're not broken because silence feels loud.
- You've just been surviving. And survival teaches us to keep moving.

But healing? Healing invites us to stop. So let me ask you, gently:

- When was the last time you sat with yourself, not to fix anything, but to listen?
- What comes up when you stop distracting, performing, or proving?
- What are you afraid you'll find in the stillness— and what might you discover instead?

You don't have to love it right away. You don't have to master it. You just have to begin. Because the version of you you're trying to become is already inside you. She's just waiting for the noise to settle long enough for you to hear her. Learning how just to *be* wasn't just about sitting still for two minutes. It was about giving myself permission to exist without having to earn it. And once

I did that—once I allowed myself to stop striving, stop fixing, stop constantly trying to measure up—everything around me started to shift. Not dramatically. Not overnight. But little by little. I stopped jumping out of bed every morning, already feeling behind. I started taking deep breaths before answering every message or request that pulled at my energy and attention. I started asking, *"Do I really want to do this?"* instead of, *"Will this make me look like I have it together?"*

Even my relationship with God began to change. For so long, I thought He needed me to perform. I felt I had to prove my faith through constant doing, serving, working, and showing up for everyone else while secretly running on empty. But in the stillness, I began to feel His presence in a way I had never felt before. Not as a taskmaster. Not as a checklist. But as a Father, quietly reminding me I was already enough. Peace didn't come because my life got easier. Peace came because I finally let go of who I thought I *had* to be—and started trusting who I already *was*. I stopped building a life that looked good and began building one that felt *true*. It wasn't always easy. Some days, I still feel the urge to hustle. To prove. To go back to what's familiar. But now I have something I didn't have before: awareness. And that awareness gives me a choice. A choice to honor my pace. A choice to pause. A choice to stay aligned with who I'm becoming, even if no one else understands it yet.

Becoming yourself doesn't require more hustle. It requires more honesty. Honesty about what hurts. About what no longer fits. About what peace feels like when you stop running long enough to notice it. I used to think rest was something I had to earn. Now I know—it's something I have to protect. I'm still learning to be okay with just being and still learning that I am valuable even in the quiet. Still unlearning the belief that I have to stay busy to be worthy. And maybe you are too. So if you find yourself in the stillness, unsure of who you are without the hustle, don't panic. That quiet space is where the real work begins. Not the work of doing, but the work of becoming and becoming is where freedom lives.

CHAPTER 4

Becoming Her

You may be thinking, "What now?" I know I was. Suddenly, I felt as though I was becoming a new person, but starting over in my thirties, TERRIFYING! However, there's good news: you're not starting from scratch; you're starting from experience. There comes a point in your journey when you've let go of so much that you're left standing in unfamiliar territory. You're no longer who you were, but not yet entirely sure of who you're becoming. It's both disorienting and liberating at the same time. That's where I found myself—somewhere between survival mode and the life I knew I was meant to live. And in that space, a quiet voice rose up in me and said, *"It's time to become her."* Not the woman the world expected me to be, but the woman I had always been beneath the noise—the one who chooses alignment, softness, strength, and peace. Becoming her wasn't a single decision. It was hundreds of small ones. Every day. And it's still unfolding. I knew who I didn't want to be anymore. But who was I now? Becoming her meant making different decisions before I fully believed I was ready. This meant saying "no" to protect my boundaries, without guilt. This meant choosing rest without trying to justify it. Hardest of all, this meant letting go of my people-pleasing ways and focusing on what I needed. Slowly but surely, I realized that each time I honored my peace, I took one step closer to 'her'.

And here's what I want you to know: *She's not some future version of you.* She's not five years away, ten pounds lighter, or only accessible once you've "healed enough." She's already inside you—right now. Beneath the burnout. Beneath the fear. Beneath the roles you've outgrown.

Becoming her doesn't require a brand-new life. It requires a brand-new level of honesty. It's the quiet decision to listen to your body instead of forcing yourself to push through. It's in the bravery of speaking your truth—even when your voice shakes. It's in the soft boundaries that protect your peace, your purpose, and your presence. Becoming her might not look loud or impressive. It might not be something anyone else claps for. But you'll feel it. In your chest. In your breath. In your *spirit*. You'll notice her in the calm that follows a hard "no." In the exhale of a Sunday afternoon where you chose to rest instead of catch up. In the joy that sneaks in when you stop proving and start *living*.

I used to think transformation had to look big. Like a leap. A rebrand. A dramatic shift that everyone could see and applaud. But becoming her didn't feel like that at all. It felt like walking into a room and not shrinking. It felt like setting my phone down and being *with* my family. It felt like finally realizing I didn't need to apologize for needing space, or rest, or joy. And some days it just looked like making it through without beating myself up. It looked like extending grace to myself when the old patterns crept back in. That's the thing about becoming her—she isn't rigid. She's not here to shame you into being better. She's here to remind you that you've *always* been enough. She just wants you to see it, too. For me, becoming her also meant redefining what success meant. I used to measure success by how busy I was. How booked I was. How much I was doing. But all that ever gave me was burnout and the aching feeling that something was still missing.

Now, success looks a lot different. It looks like peace. Like alignment. Like going to bed at night knowing I honored who I truly am—even if I didn't cross everything off the list. It's less about doing it all and more about doing what *matters*. And no, I don't have it all figured out. I still slip. I still find myself drawn back into old patterns of overgiving and overperforming. But I come back faster now. I notice sooner. I don't let shame keep me stuck. That, to me, is becoming her. Because she isn't perfect, she's present. She's soft where she used to be hardened. She's strong, not because she never falls apart, but because she no longer abandons herself when she does.

I want you to try something, and please just trust me here. This may help you, as it has me. What do you have to lose?

Take a moment and breathe. Loosen your jaw. Relax your shoulders.

Let go of the role you're carrying today—the one that says you have to be strong, capable, productive, or perfect. Now ask yourself:

- Who am I when I'm not performing?
- Who am I when I don't have to impress or please anyone?
- Who am I underneath the expectations, the deadlines, the routines?

You may not know yet. That's okay. Most of us don't at first. Because life has a way of layering identities on us like heavy coats. Wife. Mother. Provider. Leader. Helper. Fixer. Hustler. Achiever. And over time, the weight of those coats makes it hard to remember what your skin feels like underneath. But I want you to hear this:

You were someone *before* the world told you who to be.

Before the pressure.

Before the fear.

Before the striving.

And *she's still in there*.

Quiet maybe. Hidden. A little tired.

But not gone.

Becoming her isn't about changing into someone else. It's about coming back to who you already are, without all the layers of who you thought you had to be in order to be worthy.

So here's what I want you to explore, slowly, truthfully:

- What have I abandoned in myself to be accepted?
- Where in my life have I chosen peace-keeping over truth-telling?
- What parts of me feel the most silenced right now? And what are they trying to say?

You may not like the answers at first. That's okay. Truth often stings before it sets you free.

And you don't have to change everything all at once. You don't need a complete rebrand. You don't need to move across the country or start over completely. You just need to begin *returning*. Returning to your voice. Returning to your joy. Returning to your inner **knowing**—that deep intuition, that wisdom that's been quietly waiting for permission to speak again. Let this be your invitation. Not to hustle harder. Not to become perfect. But to begin tending to the woman you've neglected while taking care of everyone else. She's still here. She still matters. And she's ready to rise—not with force, but with clarity, softness, and steady intention. So ask yourself:

- What would it look like to move through this week more like her?
- How would she speak to herself when she feels behind?
- What would she let go of—not because it's bad, but because it no longer fits the woman she's becoming?

Start there. Start small. Because the becoming isn't loud. It's not about grand gestures or flashy results. It's in the pauses. The decisions made behind closed doors. The quiet boundaries no one claps for. The soft *no* that protects your peace. The honest *yes* that brings you back to life. That's where she lives. And that's where you'll find her. Not someday. But here. Now. In this quiet, courageous return to yourself.

Here are some affirmations I use almost daily to remind myself that the journey I'm on is worth it. She is worth it! Repeat these out loud. Whisper them. Write them on sticky notes. Let them settle into the spaces where doubt once lived. You don't need to *feel* them all yet. Just begin to *believe* they could be true.

I am becoming the woman I was always meant to be.

I no longer have to earn rest, love, or worth. I already am enough.

I release the need to prove myself to people who were never meant to define me.

I choose peace over pressure, and alignment over approval.

It is safe for me to slow down. It is safe for me to honor my truth.

I do not need to wait for permission to show up as my whole self

I trust the quiet steps. I trust the invisible progress. I trust the process of becoming.

Who I am becoming is not someone new—it's someone *true.*

I can carry softness and strength at the same time.

I am allowed to grow out of versions of myself that no longer fit.

I am not behind. I am not broken. I am becoming—one aligned step at a time.

BECOMING HER

You don't become her all at once. There's no grand arrival. No lightning-bolt moment when everything clicks into place and suddenly you're a brand-new woman. Becoming her is slower than that. Softer than that. More sacred than that. You become her in the small, brave choices you make every single day when you choose to rest instead of pushing, when you speak up instead of staying silent. When you honor your "no" and stop apologizing for it. When you listen to the whisper of your intuition, even when it goes against what others expect of you. You become her when you stop abandoning yourself to make others comfortable. When you finally believe that your peace is not a luxury—it's a necessity. When you realize that your worth was never up for debate to begin with, becoming her isn't about becoming perfect. It's not about being unshakable or endlessly productive. It's not about having all the answers or fixing every flaw. It's about becoming *whole*. It's about coming back to yourself. Again and again. With honesty. With gentleness. With permission to grow, to change, and to outgrow the things you once thought defined you. You already have what you need inside you. The clarity. The courage. The calling. The woman you are becoming isn't waiting for you on the other side of more effort—she's waiting for you to *remember* her. To listen to her. To trust her voice again. So when you feel lost... come back to your values. When you feel unworthy... come back to your truth. When you feel behind... come back to your *becoming*. You don't have to have it all figured out.

You just have to keep showing up—with intention, with honesty, and with love for who you are right now. Because becoming her isn't about chasing something new. It's about reclaiming what's always been yours. The version of you that's at peace with herself. Aligned with her values. Rooted in truth. Radiating freedom. That version isn't far away. She's already in you. She always has been. And now, you're finally becoming her.

CHAPTER 5

Softness is Not Weakness

"Girl, I don't know how you do it! You're so strong!"

Am I the only one who's been told this numerous times? I used to get this unhealthy ego boost from this 'compliment', but now I see it as a major red flag. I became too good at wearing burnout and hustle like a superhero cape flapping in the wind behind me as I ran full speed towards the next thing on my to-do list. I felt like being a 'supermom' and 'business woman' meant I was truly some kind of superhero, but man, does your body show you the reality with a quickness. I'm sure you've heard the saying, or maybe you haven't, "If you don't take the time to slow down, your body will make you." Welp, it is 100% true, my friends. Hate to break it to you, while you are an incredibly unique and amazing human being, that's just it. YOU'RE A HUMAN BEING! Our bodies can and will fall apart. When you wear burnout and hustle like a badge of honor, your body will eventually turn on you. And that's exactly what mine has done on multiple occasions. You would think I would've learned my lesson, but no! I'm a true, stubborn, southern woman. It took years for me to pull my head out of my ass, but thank God I finally learned.

Some say I was predisposed to this type of 'work ethic' my whole life, and I guess I can't argue. My dad is the biggest workhorse I have ever met, even with his body falling apart, literally, since he has a serious heart condition from decades of burning the candle at both ends, and my mom worked her tail off until the day she died. But why am I telling you this? Why should you care? Because living a life of hustle and grind isn't just about physically wearing yourself down. There are many emotional factors that most people tend to overlook. Somewhere along the way, hustle turns to hardness. Burnout leads to burying. Strong no longer just means grit and endurance; it becomes this facade of never showing emotions. Next thing you know, you're putting on the fake smile and using the word 'fine' to the point it has no meaning anymore, all the while you're beating on the door of your breaking point.

So no, I'm not impressed anymore when someone tells me I'm "so strong." I don't want that version of strength—the one that's just survival with lipstick on. Because what they didn't see behind that compliment was the breakdowns in the shower. The clenched jaw. The resentment boiling underneath the smile. The "I'm fine" text when I was barely holding it together. That wasn't strength. That was self-abandonment dressed in productivity. At some point, I had to ask myself:

- Why do I believe being exhausted makes me valuable?
- Why do I think numbness is proof I've made it?
- Why did I learn to equate softness with failure?

Turns out, I had absorbed this idea that softness was a liability. That crying made me fragile. That needing rest made me lazy. That showing emotion made me a mess. So I toughened up. I didn't just hustle. I hardened. And that's when I started losing pieces of myself. Not all at once—but slowly, subtly, silently. Softness wasn't just missing from my life—it was entirely unwelcome. But here's what I know now: **Softness isn't the opposite of strength. It's what allows your strength to actually *mean* something.**

I used to think being soft meant being unguarded. Unprepared. Weak. But now I see that softness is a kind of power most people are too scared to hold. Because softness asks you to feel when it would be easier to numb. It asks you to *pause* when the world demands you hustle. It asks you to stay open-hearted even after life has tried to shut you down. That takes real strength. Softness is choosing gentleness with yourself when your inner critic gets loud. It's saying no without guilt. It's allowing yourself to cry and not apologizing for it. It's taking a break before your body forces one on you. It's honoring your needs instead of constantly pushing them to the side. Softness is stillness. It's self-trust. It's that quiet voice that says, *"I don't have to carry it all."* And listen—softness doesn't mean you stop showing up. It doesn't mean you stop working hard, being reliable, or dreaming big. It means you stop sacrificing yourself in the process. It means your doing flows from alignment, not desperation. It means your strength is rooted in truth, not performance. The most resilient people I know aren't the ones who bulldoze their way through everything. They're the ones who *bend*, not break. Who knows when to push and when to rest. Who can lead and love without losing themselves. That's softness. That's wisdom. That's a strength that actually *lasts*.

I remember a morning not too long ago when everything felt like too much. The laundry was overflowing, the house was a mess, I was behind in my work, the kids were arguing, and I hadn't slept more than a couple of hours. Old me would've pushed through and poured another cup of coffee. Popped in a podcast about productivity. Told myself, *"You don't have time to fall apart today."* But that morning, I didn't push. I paused. I walked into my room, shut the door, sat on the edge of my bed, and cried. Not the quiet, controlled kind. The messy, shaking, ugly-cry kind. I let it come. I didn't try to explain it or justify it. I didn't wipe my tears and rush back into motion. I just *let myself be soft.* And something about that moment broke a pattern. I didn't feel weak. I felt *free*. Like I had finally given myself permission to be human again. That one act—sitting in stillness instead of powering through—did more for my peace than any productivity hack ever has.

My advice? Take a deep breath. Let go of the version of you that had to hold everything together. Even if just for a moment, set her down. You don't have to be "the strong one" right now. You don't have to pretend you're fine. You don't have to carry it all just to feel worthy. Let's get honest for a minute. *Where in your life are you white-knuckling your way through? Where are you saying, "I'm fine" when what you really mean is "I'm exhausted"? Where have you convinced yourself that feeling is a sign of failure?*

Perhaps you've lived in survival mode for so long that softness feels dangerous. Maybe rest feels like laziness, and crying feels like weakness. Perhaps you've learned that strength is often characterized by silence, self-sacrifice, and self-control. But what if that's not strength at all? What if real strength is showing up—honestly, fully, and vulnerably—even when it's messy? What if real strength is saying, "I'm not okay right now." "I need a break." "This is too much for me." "I don't want to do this alone anymore."

What if softness is not a liability but a superpower? A sacred reminder that you're not a machine—you're a woman with a heart, a story, and a soul that's allowed to rest. Imagine this: You give yourself permission to take a nap instead of tackling your to-do list. You cry in the shower without shame. You choose grace over grit—just for today. You look in the mirror and say, "You're doing your best. And that's enough."

Softness lives in those moments. Not in grand declarations, but in quiet returns to yourself. So ask yourself again—this time a little slower: *What would it look like to stop performing strength and start living in truth? Where could I soften—not to give up, but to give myself back to myself? What am I afraid will happen if I stop being so "strong" all the time? And what might I finally gain instead?* Softness isn't passive. It's not weakness. It's courage dressed in calm. It's presence that whispers, "I deserve to be cared for, too." And you do. Even in your stillness. Even in your tears. Even when you're not holding it all together. Especially then!

For most of my life, I believed strength meant keeping it all together. Smiling through exhaustion. Showing up even when I had nothing left to give. Proving I could handle anything—without falling apart, without asking for help, without ever slowing down. And for a while, it seemed to work until it didn't. Until the very armor I used to survive started suffocating me. Because the kind of strength I was praised for wasn't sustainable. It wasn't real. It was a costume—one I wore so well, even I forgot it was a disguise. But behind the performance, I was tired.

Tired of pretending. Tired of holding everything in. Tired of earning rest, love, and worth like they were rewards for perfect behavior. And slowly, I started to see the truth: the version of me who never showed emotion. She was never free. She was surviving. She was protecting herself from a world that taught her she had to be hard to be taken seriously. But softness—real, grounded, embodied softness—gave me everything hustle never could. It gave me peace. It gave me clarity. It gave me permission to feel, to rest, to be a whole human being instead of a perfectly polished version of one.

Softness is saying, "*I need help.*" Softness is saying, "*I'm tired.*" Softness is letting the tears come when they need to. It's choosing truth over performance. Rest over resentment. Boundaries over burnout. And it's not easy. Being soft in a hard world is a quiet kind of rebellion. It will feel unnatural at first—maybe even selfish. But it's not. It's healing. It's holy. It's necessary. So if you've been clinging to the identity of "the strong one," I invite you—gently, lovingly—to let it go. You don't have to be her anymore. Not like that. Not at the expense of yourself. Let yourself fall apart sometimes. Let yourself need. Let yourself feel the ache of years spent holding everything in—and then, let yourself breathe. Because the softest parts of you are not your weakness. They are your wisdom. They are your wholeness. They are the key to everything you've been craving. So take off the cape. Put down the heavy expectations. You don't have to be a superhero here. You just have to be *you*. Soft. Human. Worthy. Just as you are.

CHAPTER 6

Burning the Blueprint

A few years ago, in 2020, I decided it was time to pursue a career in real estate. I had thought about it for many years; even as a child, my mom dreamed of being a realtor, too. I knew the path would be challenging starting out, but I was not prepared for just how tough it would be. Y'all know what happened in 2020...COVID. The real estate market skyrocketed as interest rates plummeted to new lows. Everyone and their grandma jumped at the chance to be real estate agents. You couldn't throw a rock without hitting an agent, at least in my area. It was insane! Not only was I new, but now I was literally one of thousands. Standing out just got that much harder.

So, I did what I always did back then, before working on myself, and hustled even harder. It took me almost a full year, but I finally got my first client. I was over the moon excited. We made it to closing, and they got the keys to their first house...yay! My commission check came in, and

I was dancing. I thought I would ride that high forever. But it only took a few days before I found myself chasing after the next 'high'. It wasn't until I had gotten a few more that I realized something that shook me to my core. I thought reaching that milestone would make me feel successful. It didn't. It just made me realize how far I'd drifted from myself.

I had done everything "right." I set the goal, put in the work, grinded through the slow season, pushed past the doubt, and I got the win. And yet... it didn't feel like I thought it would. Yes, I was proud of myself. Yes, I was grateful. But underneath the surface, I felt something else I couldn't shake: emptiness. Not because I didn't love helping my clients—I did. Not because I didn't appreciate the income—I definitely did. But because I was starting to realize I had tied my sense of value to a moving target. I thought the next closing would finally make me feel "enough." I thought if I just hit the next milestone, I'd finally feel fulfilled. But every win faded faster than the one before. That was the moment I started to question everything. *Whose version of success am I chasing? What blueprint am I following—and who even wrote it?* When I looked closer, I saw it: I was still trying to prove something. To myself. To my family. To the world.

I wanted to be seen as the strong one. The one who made it. The one who hustled and built something out of nothing. But the truth was I was building a life that looked successful, but didn't feel like mine. That realization hit me hard. Because I wasn't just chasing closings. I was chasing validation. I was chasing identity. I was chasing worth in the form of approval and productivity. That's when I knew that the blueprint I had been handed—work hard, stay busy, prove your value through performance—it wasn't working for me anymore. So I lit the match. Let me be clear: I didn't burn everything down in one day. But the moment I realized I was living by someone else's definition of success, I couldn't unsee it. I had spent years following an invisible checklist:

- Hustle hard
- Be "on" all the time.
- Say yes, even when you're drowning.
- Keep it together no matter what.
- Measure your worth by your output.

Sound familiar? It wasn't written on paper, but it was everywhere—in my upbringing, in the culture I was raised in, in the subtle messages passed down through family, faith, and the business world. Work hard, and eventually you'll be happy. Push through, and eventually it'll pay off. Don't rest—there's too much to do. But it never stopped. The goalposts always moved. And I realized I was building a life that checked every box... except the ones that actually mattered to me. So I started burning things down. I stopped glamorizing burnout. I stopped saying yes just to be seen as "reliable." I stopped ignoring my body, my needs, and my peace in the name of being "driven." I even started questioning the way I measured success entirely. And let me tell you—it wasn't graceful. There were moments I panicked. Moments I thought, *What if I'm throwing away everything I've worked for? What if I'm quitting?* But here's the truth:

I wasn't quitting.

I was choosing.

Choosing *me*. Choosing alignment. Choosing peace over pressure. Choosing a life that felt like mine, not one that just looked impressive to other people. Burning the blueprint meant grieving an identity I had clung to for years. It meant facing the fear of being misunderstood, disappointing people, or appearing as though I'd lost my ambition. But the more profound fear—the one I could no longer ignore—was what might happen if I *didn't* burn it. What would happen to my health, my relationships, my spirit... if I kept building a life that didn't fit?

So I let it burn.

The old rules.

The outdated definitions.

The polished image.

The pressure to prove anything to anyone.

And from the ashes, I finally had space to ask a better question: *What does success actually mean to me, now, in this season, as the woman I'm becoming?*

When I burned the old blueprint, I wasn't left empty. I was left *open*. Open to a new way of thinking. Open to rebuilding a definition of success that *felt* good. One that honored who I was, not who I thought I had to be to be worthy. And at first I didn't even know where to start. Because for so long, success was defined by numbers:

- How many closings.
- How much money.
- How many hours I worked.
- How many people needed me.

But now success looks and feels *completely different*. Success is waking up with peace in my chest, rather than panic. Success is saying *no* without spiraling into guilt. Success is building a business that doesn't burn me out. Success is having time to sit down and eat with my family without checking my phone. Success is alignment. It's when my calendar reflects my values. It's when my goals are rooted in purpose, not pressure. It's when my work flows from who I am, not who I'm trying to prove myself to be. And guess what? Success can still include growth. It can still include achievement, income, impact, and ambition. But now, those things are *outcomes*, not the foundation. They're fruit from a life that's rooted in clarity and intention. I no longer chase success the way I used to. Now, I *create* it. Every time I honor my boundaries. Every time I protect my peace. Every time I trust my intuition instead of defaulting to the grind. That is success. And it's available to you, too, not once you do enough, prove enough, or achieve enough. But the moment you decide that your *definition* matters more than anyone else's expectations. You don't need to perform for your peace. You don't need to hustle your way into being enough. You are allowed to want a version of success that *feels like home*. And that version? It's probably quieter. Softer. More spacious. More *you*.

Redefining success didn't happen overnight. At first, it felt like I was walking around in the dark, unsure of what to aim for, what to celebrate, or what to be proud of. I was so used to chasing the "next big thing" that slowing down to ask, *"What do I actually want?"* felt awkward... even selfish. But I kept asking. And slowly, my answers changed. I stopped needing external validation to feel like I was doing something meaningful. I stopped associating exhaustion with accomplishment. And I started listening to what *felt* right instead of what looked good on paper. And yes, it was uncomfortable. There were days I second-guessed myself. Days I wondered if I had lost my drive. Days when I saw others "winning" in ways I used to crave and thought, *Should I want that again?* But then I'd catch myself sitting on the couch with my kids, not rushing to the next task, just present. Just *here*. Or I'd finish a workday without anxiety lingering in my chest. Or I'd say no to something that used to cost me my peace, and feel *relief* instead of guilt. And I'd remember: This is what success feels like *now*. It's in the little moments most people overlook. The quiet joy. The sustainable pace. The freedom to choose your own priorities. It's in the shift from proving to *being*. From surviving to *savoring*. Success is alignment. Success is integrity with your values. Success is a day that feels like it belongs to *you*, not to someone else's checklist. Sometimes, it still feels weird to celebrate this version of success, because it's not flashy. It's not always impressive to the outside world. But it's *freeing*. And I'll take peace over pressure any day.

One of the biggest shifts I had to make, but also the most rewarding, was learning to celebrate the small wins—the ones no one sees. The quiet ones. The ones that don't get likes or praise or income attached to them. Because success, as I used to know it, was loud. It was always about the *next big thing*. The next goal, the next check, the next opportunity. And if it didn't move the needle or show up on paper it didn't "count." But that version of success nearly wrecked me. Because while I was chasing big wins, I was missing the sacred ones. I wasn't celebrating the moments when I stayed calm, even when I wanted to snap. I wasn't proud of the days I chose rest instead of pushing through. I wasn't giving myself credit for setting boundaries, protecting my peace, or simply surviving a hard day with grace. But those are wins, too. In fact, those are the wins that *matter most*. So I started shifting the way I measured growth. Instead of just asking, *What did I accomplish today?* I started asking: *What did I honor today? What did I protect? Where did I choose alignment over approval? What would the woman I'm becoming be proud of in this moment?*

And the answers were quieter, but so much more meaningful. Sometimes, success looks like putting your phone away during dinner. Sometimes, it's canceling a meeting because your body is tired and your soul is louder than your calendar. Sometimes, it's having the hard conversation you've been avoiding—and doing it with softness and clarity. Sometimes, it's going to bed on time. Drinking water. Saying "I'm not okay." I started calling these *micro-wins*. Tiny, intentional acts of self-respect. Little, often-unseen moments that said: *I'm not abandoning myself anymore.* And let me tell you—when you string those micro-wins together, they change everything. They shift your energy. They shape your identity. They help you *become* the woman you're trying to build everything for in the first place. You don't need a massive milestone to validate your growth. Sometimes, the smallest decisions can lead to the biggest transformations. And when you start living like that you realize success was never out there waiting for you. It was in you all along, waiting to be *redefined*.

Humor me again and close your eyes. Imagine, just for a minute, that you let go of the pressure to keep up, to measure up, to prove yourself one more time. This is your invitation to pause and ask yourself what you're really chasing. Because the world will hand you a hundred ways to define success. It'll tell you it's in the numbers, the pace, the image, the hustle. But what if you don't want any of that? What if your version of success is quieter, but deeper? Maybe success for you is:

- Waking up without anxiety buzzing in your chest
- Feeling proud of a boundary you kept
- Hearing your child say, "You weren't on your phone today"
- Finally listening to your gut over your guilt
- Choosing peace over perfection

That counts. That matters. That *is* success. You're allowed to want a life that feels good on the inside—even if it looks slower, softer, or smaller from the outside. So ask yourself:

- Where have I been measuring my worth with someone else's ruler?
- What if I stopped chasing—and started living?
- What would success look like if it weren't about performance, but presence?

Here's what I know now: The success that actually matters is the kind you feel in your chest, not just in your bank account. It's the kind that lets you breathe, not just produce. It's the kind that honors your values, protects your peace, and still leaves room for joy. You don't need to chase it. You just need to define it for *yourself*. And once you do, you'll stop living to impress others. You'll start living in integrity with yourself. That's when everything changes. That's when you realize—You're not behind. You're not lost. You're just redefining success. And for the first time, it actually *fits*.

CHAPTER 7

The Rise of the Real You

I thought I had done the work. I had slowed down and started resting. Reclaimed my values. Burned the damn blueprint. I had finally stopped saying "yes" to things that drained me and even learned how to sit in stillness without unraveling. So, naturally, I assumed I was done performing. But one morning, I opened Instagram, selected a photo, and started writing a caption that felt... honest, not curated. Not sugar-coated. Not "on brand." Just *real*. I paused, then deleted the entire thing. My brain instantly scrambled:

That's too much.

What will people think?

This might sound unprofessional.

Maybe I should just share a quote instead.

And there it was—performance. Hiding. Filtering. Even after all that healing, I was still trying to manage how I was seen. I wasn't lying... but I also wasn't telling the whole truth. I wasn't being fake... but I also wasn't being *free*. That moment hit me hard, not because I cared about Instagram, but because I realized how often I was still shrinking. Still asking:

- Is this too bold?
- Is this too emotional?
- Is this too honest?
- Am *I* too much?

It was a gut punch—because I had worked so hard to reclaim my peace... and yet I was still afraid to be seen in it. Not a new version of me. The *real* me. The one who laughs too loudly. Cries when she's passionate. Uses the f-word and still prays hard. The one who is no longer hustling to be everything for everyone, but still catching herself apologizing for not trying. And I knew in that moment: the next part of the journey wasn't about slowing down or aligning my life. It was about *showing up in it*. Unfiltered. Unedited. Unapologetic. Not because I needed to prove anything. But because I was tired of hiding the parts of me that were already whole.

Being real isn't about baring your soul on social media. It's not about oversharing. It's not about mess for the sake of "relatability." Being real is about *honesty*, starting with yourself. It's about showing up in your life without constantly editing who you are to be more digestible. It's about letting your truth take up space, even if it makes someone uncomfortable. Even if it scares you a little. For most of my life, I thought being "real" was something you earned. Like once you were healed enough, confident enough, sure enough, you'd finally have permission to be your whole self. However, I've learned it doesn't work that way. You don't wait until you're fully ready. You *practice* being real until it starts to feel safe. Being real isn't always loud. Sometimes, it's the quietest thing you do. It's pausing before you say "yes" and asking yourself, *Do I actually want this?* It's posting the photo that doesn't hide your wrinkles. It's admitting that you're not okay without rushing to explain or apologize for it. It's taking up space in a room you used to shrink in. Being real is also tender. Because the moment you stop performing, you feel everything more. The fear of being judged. The risk of being misunderstood. The ache of not being liked by everyone. But also... the freedom. The relief. The *honesty* of not pretending anymore. Being real isn't about throwing away your boundaries or walking around emotionally exposed all the time. It's not about being unfiltered to prove something. It's about *alignment*. Letting the version of you the world sees match the one you've been becoming behind the scenes. And that— more than any title, role, or performance—is where your power lives. Not in how polished you are. Not in how productive you are. But in how *true* you're willing to be. Because when you show up as your whole self, you stop hustling for belonging. You create it.

And here's the thing no one tells you: Being real can feel incredibly lonely at first.

When you stop pretending, some people stop clapping. When you stop overgiving, some people stop asking. When you stop performing, some people start pulling away. And that hurts. It's disorienting to realize how much of your relationships were built on the version of you who was always available, always agreeable, always "fine." But the truth is—those relationships weren't built on *you*. They were built on your performance. And you deserve more than that. You deserve connections where you can exhale, where you can speak your truth without having to walk it back. Where you don't have to smile through disappointment just to keep the peace. Being real might cost you approval. But it will give you *peace*. And peace is worth everything. It will also attract the *right* people. The ones who don't flinch at your honesty. The ones who don't shrink when you rise. The ones who say, "Same, me too," instead of "Whoa, tone it down." Because when you show up as your authentic self, something incredible happens: you stop performing connection and start experiencing it. Deep, honest, mutual connection—the kind that doesn't require a mask or a perfectly timed smile. And once you taste that kind of freedom...You'll never want to go back to the filtered version of your life again.

I remember a time—not that long ago—when I walked into a room and immediately shrank. Not because anyone said anything. Not because I wasn't qualified to be there. But because I had trained myself to scan the space first... and shape-shift second. I adjusted my tone. I kept my opinions polite. I smiled a little too much. I made sure not to take up too much space. I told myself it was "professional." Really, it was just fear. Fear of being seen too clearly. Fear of being misunderstood. Fear of being too loud, too messy, too *much*. That version of me knew how to keep things smooth, agreeable, and acceptable. But she didn't know how to feel safe being *real*.

Now? Now I walk into rooms a little differently. I still get nervous. I still notice the urge to shrink. But I breathe deeper. I ground myself. I remind myself: *You don't have to shape-shift to be safe anymore. You're allowed to belong as you are.*

And when I speak now it's not to be impressive. It's to be honest. When I take up space now it's not to dominate. It's to *occupy* the space I already deserve to hold. And it's wild—how different everything feels when you stop performing for approval and start showing up for *yourself*. I'm still learning and still unlearning. I still catch myself in old patterns sometimes. But I'm also catching glimpses of the real me, and I like her. Not because she's polished. But because she's finally free.

Have you ever lived in survival mode? I know I'm guilty of that on more than one occasion. It happens so stealthily and subtly that it's almost impossible to see it happening. Here's the thing about survival mode: it doesn't ask for your truth. It asks for your obedience. It asks, *What do I need to be right now to stay safe, accepted, needed, approved of?* And little by little, that question shapes who you become. You learn to read the room before you speak. You learn to overdeliver so no one ever questions your value. You learn to smile when you're hurting, keep going when you're breaking, and say "yes" when everything in you is screaming "no." You become adaptable. Efficient. High-functioning. You get good at being everything for everyone, except yourself.

But none of that is the real you. That's the *survival version* of you. The one who did what she had to do. The one who got you through. And let me pause right here and say—she deserves *so much* credit. She protected you. She got things done. She kept the peace. She made sure you were accepted, liked, maybe even applauded. She played her part, and she played it well. But now? Now you're safe enough to stop performing. You're aware enough to choose differently. And the version of you that's rising doesn't want to perform anymore. She wants to be *free*. That means grieving the masks and releasing the roles.

Thanking the woman who helped you survive, while making space for the one who's here to *live*. Because beneath all that proving, fixing, overfunctioning, and people-pleasing... There's someone softer. Someone bolder. Someone more honest. Someone more whole. And she's not here to just get through the day. She's here to *belong* in it. Fully. Without needing to shrink or shape-shift ever again.

Can we be honest for a minute here? It's not always the becoming that's hard—it's the *being seen* in it. Being seen for who you are—without the polish, the pretense, the perfect answers—is terrifying. Because deep down, we've been taught that visibility is a risk. That if someone sees the real you—the raw you—the unsure, emotional, too-much, too-loud, too-soft you—they might leave. And that fear is not dramatic. It's *true to your experience*. Perhaps you were teased when you were sensitive. Maybe your confidence was labeled "bossy." Maybe your needs were too much for someone you trusted. Possibly the last time you let someone in, they walked away. Or worse—they stayed, but only loved the version of you that made them comfortable. So you started editing yourself. Not because you're weak, but because you're *human*. And all humans long for connection and belonging. But here's the trap: The connection you build by shrinking yourself will always be fragile because it's not a real connection. Its performance. The truth is that being fully seen is a risk. But it's the only path to being fully loved. Because when you're hiding, any approval you receive is only hitting the mask, not you. And deep down, you *know* that, which is why it never feels like enough.

That's the ache you can't shake. The one that says, *"If they really knew me... would they still love me?"* And maybe they wouldn't. But maybe... *they would*. And not just love you, but *see you*. Honor you. Celebrate you. But you'll never know until you stop hiding. Being fully seen isn't easy. It will make your voice shake. It will feel like exposure. But it's also where *real freedom* lives. And maybe you don't go from zero to complete vulnerability overnight. Maybe being seen starts small. Like saying, "Actually, I don't agree with that." Like hitting "post" on something that's genuinely yours. Like letting someone in on what you're really feeling instead of just saying, "I'm fine." Like not apologizing for your truth, even if it makes someone uncomfortable. Every time you let yourself be seen, you build evidence: *It's safe to be real. I survived that. I'm still here.* And one day, you'll look around and realize—you're not just surviving anymore. You're finally living. Unhidden. Unfiltered. Unapologetically yourself.

I remember sitting in my car outside of a meeting I had agreed to weeks before—one of those "networking opportunities" I used to say yes to without question. The kind where I'd show up looking polished, smile through my exhaustion, and pretend I was fine, productive, and excited to be there—even if I wasn't.

But on this day, something felt different. I sat in the driver's seat, hands on the wheel, staring at the building in front of me, and I just... *paused*. Everything in me wanted to override the discomfort. To power through. To do what I always did—show up, perform, be the "good girl" who follows through no matter what it costs. But I didn't. Instead, I let the silence stretch out. I checked in with myself. And what I heard was clear: *"You don't want to go in there. And you don't have to."*

It wasn't fear speaking. It wasn't self-sabotage. It was *clarity*. I didn't want to go because the version of me who said yes to that meeting had done it out of obligation, not alignment. Out of fear of missing out. Out of fear of disappointing someone. Out of fear that if I didn't stay "visible," I'd fall behind. But the real me? The *current* me? She knew that peace mattered more than proving. She knew that forcing herself into a room she didn't belong in wasn't brave—it was *exhausting*. So I drove away. I didn't explain. I didn't send a lengthy apology via text. I didn't punish myself later. I just chose myself. Quietly. And I'm sure some of you reading this may be thinking, "Now that's just rude," but let me tell you, something about that moment felt like a revolution. Because for the first time in a long time, I didn't abandon myself for optics. I didn't shrink my knowing to fit someone else's expectations. I listened to the real me, and I let her lead. That's what reclaiming can look like. Not loud. Not dramatic. Just honest. And that kind of decision? That's when you start to feel free—not just on the outside, but in your *bones*.

There comes a point in your healing when you don't just reflect on who you've been—you start remembering who you've always been. Not the survival version. Not the edited version. Not the version crafted to meet everyone else's needs. But the *real* you. The one who used to light up when she talked about her dreams. The one who laughed loudly and didn't care who heard her. The one who had opinions, feelings, boundaries, and didn't apologize for any of them. The one who *felt at home* in her own skin. You start to notice her again in the smallest ways:

- In the way your shoulders relax when you say "no" without guilt.
- In the way your voice feels steady when you speak your truth.
- In the joy that bubbles up when you stop overthinking and just *be*.

And reclaiming her? It's sacred. It means gathering the pieces of yourself that you gave away to be accepted. It means welcoming back the parts of you that were "too much" for someone else. It means finally allowing yourself to *belong* to yourself. You might find you're more sensitive than you let on. More bold. More creative. More opinionated. More intuitive. More tender. More fiery. Maybe you were taught those things were weaknesses.

Perhaps you tucked them away to make them easier to love. But they were never the problem. They were always your power. You don't need to explain why you want them back. You don't need permission to reclaim them. You just get to say, *'This is mine.' And I'm done leaving her behind.* The real you doesn't need fixing. She needs freedom. Freedom to be complex. Freedom to be seen. Freedom to evolve and expand, and no longer make herself smaller just to stay digestible. This isn't about becoming someone new. It's about finally choosing to be someone *true.*

The truth is, the real you was never gone. She didn't disappear. She didn't break. She just got buried beneath everything you thought you had to be. The roles. The pressure. The expectations. The performance. But now? Now you're remembering.

Every time you honor your truth instead of hiding it...

Every time you choose rest over proving...

Every time you speak up when it would be easier to stay quiet...

Every time you soften instead of harden just to survive another day...

You're rising. Not as someone new. But as someone *true.* You're not behind. You're not starting over. You're becoming who you were always meant to be—before life, fear, or survival taught you to forget. So take this chapter as your reminder: You don't need to perform to be powerful. You don't need to be perfect to be worthy. You don't need to be liked by everyone to be aligned with yourself. You are allowed to be fully seen. You are allowed to take up space. You are allowed to choose *you*, over and over again. Because the world doesn't need more perfect women, it needs more *honest* ones. More women living their truth, even if their voice shakes. More women who show up unfiltered, unapologetic, and unafraid to be *fully themselves*. And if you're still figuring out who that is—that's okay. You don't have to know it all to rise. You just have to be willing to stop hiding. To stop shrinking. To stop performing for a version of success, love, or approval that was never meant for you in the first place. The real you is not too much. She's just been waiting for you to finally come home.

Let her rise.

CHAPTER 8

Unlearning the Lies

You've been becoming the real you. But to truly live as her, you need to unlearn the internalized lies that have been keeping you small, even subconsciously. These lies are the invisible scripts that still whisper:

"You have to earn your worth."

"You're too emotional."

"You'll be rejected if you show too much."

"Peace is selfish."

"Rest is laziness."

"You have to be needed to be loved."

You don't just break free by building a new identity. You break free by challenging the old stories. My biggest struggle with this is the lie of guilt and laziness. More specifically, when I choose to rest instead of work or, dare

I say, play with my kids. I know that both are necessary, but I have to remind myself that each has its place in my life. Just as I can't work all the time, I also can't play with my kids all the time. I have had to start reframing my thoughts about resting, especially when I choose it over things that also seem important. I have to work to earn a living. My kids desire a loving mom who plays with them every day. But, just as the dishes eventually have to be done, the laundry needs to be washed, and the trash needs to be taken out, I need to rest. But my brain likes to try to make me believe that when I'm resting, I'm lazy. It also LOVES to play the guilt card about resting over playing with my kids.

Even now, after all the work I've done to reclaim peace and alignment, I still find myself in these internal battles. I'll be sitting on the couch, coffee in hand, taking a breath—and my brain will whisper:

You should be folding laundry.

You should be writing that thing.

You should be playing with your kids. They won't be this little forever.

And suddenly, what started as a sacred pause becomes a guilt-ridden spiral. Not because I don't care about my responsibilities—of course I do. But because I've spent years being conditioned to believe that stillness is selfish.

That if I'm not doing something for someone else, I'm falling short. It's taken real, intentional work to reframe that. To remind myself that I am not lazy—I am human, that I can love my job and still need rest. That I can be a devoted mother and *still have limits*. Choosing rest isn't choosing *against* anyone else. It's choosing to be whole *with* myself. And yes, the dishes will need to be done. Yes, the kids will still want my attention. Yes, the to-do list will continue to grow. But so will my resentment—if I keep pouring from a dry, brittle place. So now, when the guilt creeps in, I speak a different truth over it: *Rest is not a reward. It's a requirement. And I'm allowed to be a good mom, a good woman, a good human, without being exhausted all the time.* I'm not lazy. I'm not selfish. I'm just unlearning the lie that said I had to earn my worth.

The lies aren't always loud. In fact, they're usually quiet. Subtle. Familiar. They sound just enough like responsibility, just enough like love, just enough like ambition to keep you believing them.

They don't say, *"You're not enough."*

They say, *"You should be doing more."*

They don't say, *"You're failing."*

They say, *"Don't let anyone down."*

They don't scream, *"You're lazy."*

They whisper, *"Must be nice to rest. Must be nice to have time."*

And because they sound so close to logic... you don't always question them. You just obey. You keep moving. Keep giving. Keep producing. Keep proving. Because anything less starts to feel like weakness. But let's be honest—what kind of life does that create? You start measuring your worth by your productivity. You start believing that your presence isn't enough unless it's *doing* something for someone else. You stop asking yourself what *you* need, because you're too busy anticipating what everyone else might. And before you know it, you've built a life around false urgency. A life that looks responsible, selfless, maybe even impressive—but underneath it all, you're exhausted. Empty. Resentful. Disconnected. Not just from others, but from *yourself.* And it's not because you're broken. It's because you've been lied to. Lies like:

"Good moms never say no."

"If you don't do it, no one else will."

"They'll think you're selfish if you rest."

"You can relax when everything's done." (Spoiler: it's never all done.)

"You should be grateful—others have it worse."

"Don't waste time. You need to stay ahead."

Sound familiar? These thoughts don't just weigh you down—they steal your presence. Your joy. Your clarity. Your peace. But here's the truth: **Your worth doesn't increase when your to-do list is complete. And it doesn't decrease when your body needs a break.**

You are allowed to say:

"This can wait."

"I need a moment."

"My needs matter, too."

That's not laziness. That's liberation.

I recall a specific day when the guilt hit me harder than usual. It had been a long week full of work deadlines, errands, a sick kid, and barely any sleep. My body was tired in that bone-deep way that no amount of coffee could fix. All I wanted was to sit down for twenty minutes. Just breathe. Maybe read a few pages of a book or close my eyes while the house was still quiet. But as soon as I curled up on the couch, my youngest ran in, holding his arts and crafts box and smiling widely.

"Mommy, will you play with me?"

Instant tension. My heart wanted to say yes. My body screamed no. But before I could even think it through, the lie kicked in full force:

"You're already behind."

"You haven't spent enough time with him this week."

"This might be the moment he remembers forever, and you're choosing rest?"

"You'll regret this later."

So I smiled. I sat at the table and began to listen to what we would be creating. Sadly, the whole time I was sitting there, I wasn't present. I was resentful. Snapping at misplaced scissors. Half-listening. Half there. I didn't give him a joyful version of me. I gave him a drained shell of myself—all because I believed I wasn't *allowed* to rest first. After he went to bed that night, I cried. Not because I didn't love him—God, I love him more than anything. But because I hated the version of me that was showing up: Scattered. Worn down. Resentful when I wanted to be present. Snapping when I wanted to laugh. That's what the lie of guilt steals from us. Not just energy, but *connection*. It tells us that self-sacrifice equals love, when in reality, sacrificing your well-being often robs the people you love of your whole self. I thought choosing him meant denying me. But now I know: choosing *me* first would've allowed me to choose *him* better. That was a turning point. A moment I promised myself: I won't trade presence for performance anymore. Because what he needs most isn't a perfect mom. He needs a *whole* one. And I can't be whole if I'm always running on empty. That moment taught me something I hadn't put words to yet: Wholeness doesn't begin with doing more. It starts with noticing *why* you're doing anything at all. That's when I realized:

Maybe freedom doesn't come from finally getting it all right.

It may start by questioning the beliefs that have been running the show.

The first step to freedom isn't pushing harder; it's pausing long enough to notice what's guiding your choices. Because the lies are sneaky. They sound like discipline. They feel like responsibility. They masquerade as love, ambition, excellence, and even faith.

Here's what I've learned:

Anything that guilts you into self-abandonment is not love.

Anything that shames you out of rest is not the truth.

And anything that equates your worth with your output is a damn lie.

And the only way to stop obeying the lies... is to start *replacing* them. So I started doing something simple—but powerful: I named the lie. And I wrote down the truth. At first, it felt small. But over time it changed everything.

Here are a few lies I've had to unlearn—and the truths I've chosen to replace them with:

The Lie	The Truth
"If I don't do it, no one will."	I am not the only capable person. Delegating is wise, not weak.
"I can rest when everything is done."	The to-do list will never end. Rest is part of doing well.
"They'll think I'm selfish."	People's assumptions are not my responsibility. I can honor my needs without guilt.
"If I say no, I'll disappoint them."	A short-term no protects long-term peace—for both of us.
"I'm lazy if I sit down."	I'm human. Rest is not laziness—it's leadership of self.
"Being needed makes me valuable."	My value isn't in being needed. It's in being me. Fully, honestly, and freely.

Now, when the lie creeps in—and it still does—I pause. I breathe. And I say, *"That's the old story. I don't live there anymore."* It's not always easy. Some days, the lie still feels louder than the truth. But the difference now? I know which voice is mine. And I trust her more.

If no one has told you this yet, let me be the first:

> You are not behind.
>
> You are not lazy.
>
> You are not too much, nor are you not enough.
>
> You are not selfish for needing rest.
>
> You are not failing because you feel overwhelmed.
>
> You are not broken.

You were just lied to by a culture that glorifies burnout and calls it ambition. Lied to by systems that value your productivity more than your presence. Lied to by people who only loved you when you were easy to manage, easy to please, easy to applaud. Lied to by old versions of yourself that were just doing their best to survive. But here you are—choosing to unlearn. To get quiet. To listen closely. To return to your truth. And that's holy work. Because once you start noticing the lies, you start reclaiming your life. You stop saying "yes" because you're afraid to say "no." You stop apologizing for your energy, your voice, your limits. You stop measuring your worth by how busy you are or how much you've done. And you start living differently. You start honoring your body when it whispers, "*Slow down.*" You start protecting your peace as if it were priceless—because it is. You start showing up in rooms with your whole truth, not just the digestible parts. You start resting without guilt. You begin laughing again—loud, messy, unfiltered. You start trusting that your life doesn't have to look like anyone else's to be worthy. And when those old lies try to creep back in—and they will—you'll have a new voice inside you that says:

"No, not today. That story has expired. I know who I am now."

This is what unlearning looks like. It's not a single moment of clarity—it's a thousand quiet decisions to choose truth over fear. To choose alignment over approval. To choose peace over performance. To choose *yourself*, not in a self-centered way, but in a soul-centered way. And maybe the most challenging part of it all? Forgiving yourself for the years you spent believing the lies. Not because you were weak, but because you were never taught anything different. But you know now. And that knowing? It's freedom. It's strength. It's power.

So here's your permission—not that you ever needed it:

You are allowed to rest.

You are allowed to say no.

You are allowed to be soft.

You are allowed to stop performing.

You are allowed to take up space.

You are allowed to unlearn every lie that ever told you otherwise.

Because the truth is this: You've never been unworthy. You've just been unkind to yourself for too long. And now? Now you're done living a life built on fear, guilt, and false stories. Now... you're writing a new one. Page by page. Choice by choice. Truth by truth. Not to prove anything. But to finally live.

CHAPTER 9

Trusting Yourself Again (Even When the Old You Shows Up)

Have you ever made a commitment to yourself, even something small, and then felt like crap when you didn't follow through? Something as simple as, "I'm going to wake up early tomorrow", but then hit snooze again? I have, many times. I beat myself up with guilt and then usually give up. Because it's never just about hitting snooze, is it? It's about what that tiny moment says to your brain: *See? We never follow through. We don't do what we say we're going to do.* And it stacks. Quietly. Every small broken promise starts to build a case against your reliability. Until one day, you realize you don't trust yourself to show up anymore—not with discipline, not with rest, not with dreams, not even with something as small as water before coffee.

I remember one afternoon when I had promised myself I'd rest—just one hour—no phone, no tasks, just quiet.

But as soon as I sat down, the guilt hit—the laundry called. The emails blinked. A client needed something. I told myself, "Just ten minutes to catch up," and before I knew it, the whole hour was gone. The worst part wasn't skipping rest. It was the message I sent to myself: "You don't matter as much as the list." That realization hit hard. And it wasn't the first time. I had made a habit of betraying my own needs and calling it discipline. I realized that each time you tell yourself you're going to do something and don't do it, you're losing trust in yourself. Yikes! It makes sense, but it's still unsettling to think about. Just as when someone we know goes back on their commitments and we begin to lose trust in them, when we go back on our own, we lose confidence in ourselves. And here's what makes that so heavy: You start to doubt your word, not just to others, but to yourself. You hesitate before making any decision. You get stuck in a cycle of overthinking, procrastination, guilt, and shame. You avoid setting goals altogether because deep down, you're afraid you won't follow through anyway. It's not laziness—it's *grief*. Grief from all the times you've abandoned yourself, trying to keep everything else together.

I don't know about you, but when I realized this, I was *shook*. I started wondering how I could possibly regain trust in myself after all the years of broken promises. It felt overwhelming at first. Like, how do you start over with someone who's let you down over and over again... when that someone is you?

Here's the secret: each time you choose yourself, uphold a boundary, or say 'no' to something to protect your peace, you're building your trust back in yourself. It's a slow process, but the trust does build. But don't be surprised once you start to accumulate that trust and the old you shows up. The one who overcommits out of guilt. The one who says "yes" when she's already overwhelmed. The one who breaks her boundaries to keep the peace. The one who *really* wants to believe she's healed, but panics the moment someone is disappointed. At first, I was so frustrated. I thought, *"Seriously? I thought we were past this."* But healing doesn't mean the old patterns vanish. It means you finally have the awareness to *choose differently* when they show up. Because that version of you—the overachiever, the people-pleaser, the woman who didn't know she was allowed to rest—she's not your enemy. She's just a part of you that learned to survive. A part that believed: *if I don't do it all, I'm not enough.*

So when she comes back around, that doesn't mean you've failed. It just means your nervous system is asking: **"Are we really safe to live this way now?"**

That's your opportunity to answer:

Yes.

We're safe.

We're allowed to rest.

We're allowed to say no.

We're allowed to trust ourselves again.

Because rebuilding self-trust doesn't happen in the perfectly aligned days, it occurs in the shaky ones—the ones where you catch yourself mid-pattern, mid-people-pleasing, mid-spiral—and choose another way.

Here's what I had to learn the hard way:

You don't rebuild trust in yourself with one big breakthrough. You rebuild it with **tiny, quiet, consistent decisions** that say, "*I'm safe with me now.*"

That means:

Keeping small promises—even when no one's watching. Saying no *without* writing a novel explaining why. Taking a break before you're on the edge of burnout. Letting your "I need rest" carry just as much weight as "I need to get things done." Showing up for *you* the way you've shown up for everyone else.

At first, it might feel silly. Too small to matter. But those small acts? They're sacred. Because for years, you taught yourself that your needs could wait. That your body could wait. That *you* could wait. Now, every time you choose you—without guilt—you're rewriting the story. Let me be clear: this is not about perfection. You will still hit snooze. You will still cancel workouts, miss deadlines, and forget to drink your water. That doesn't mean you've failed. It means you're human. What matters is what you do next. Do you spiral into shame? Or do you say, *"That's okay. Let's try again tomorrow."* That moment? That's the muscle. That's the work. That's the trust being rebuilt.

Every time you follow through on a boundary...

Every time you rest without over-explaining...

Every time you check in with yourself *before* checking your phone...

You're teaching yourself something powerful:

"You can count on me now."

That self-trust is the root of everything you're building.

You don't have to fix everything today. You don't need to earn your way back into self-trust. You just need to begin—slowly, honestly, and without shame. Take a breath. Loosen your shoulders. Put your hand on your heart if it helps. Now ask yourself:

- Where have I stopped trusting myself—and why?
- What's one area of my life where I constantly override my own needs?
- What lie do I tend to believe when I don't follow through?

- What truth do I want to start practicing instead?

And then ask:

- What's one **small, doable** promise I can keep to myself this week?

(Not to prove anything—but to build trust.)

A walk outside

Drinking one glass of water before coffee

Saying "no" without explaining

Taking five minutes before bed just for you

Speaking your truth, even if your voice shakes

Let it be small. Let it be enough. You don't build self-trust by doing more.

You build it by *showing up with integrity to your truth*. One honest yes. One clear no. One pause instead of a people-pleasing reflex. That's how the foundation gets rebuilt. And here's the most important part:

When you mess up—and you will—*be kind*.

The way you speak to yourself in the mess matters more than how perfect you were trying to be. Self-trust isn't built in perfection. It's built on the grace you give yourself every time you try again. Trusting myself changed everything—not overnight, but slowly, deeply, and permanently. It changed how I show up in my work, motherhood, and in my marriage. It changed how I hear myself and how I forgive myself. I no longer need to earn peace. I just need to return to it.

One aligned decision. One kept promise. One brave, quiet choice at a time.

CHAPTER 10

Where She Begins

You made it.

Not to the end of the work, but to the beginning of something honest. Something aligned. Something yours. You've walked through the lies, the burnout, the blueprints you were never meant to follow. You've unlearned who the world told you to be. You've begun remembering the woman underneath the noise. You've wrestled with guilt. You've chosen softness in a world that demanded you stay hard. You've paused instead of pushing. You've said "no" without writing a novel to explain it. And maybe for the first time, you believed yourself when you said, "I deserve more than this." Maybe you're still scared. Maybe you still doubt. Maybe there's a part of you that wonders if you'll slip back into the old patterns. Let me tell you something: You will. There will be days when your nervous system craves the familiar, when people-pleasing feels easier than peace-keeping, when your old survival tools show up like old friends offering comfort. Not because you've failed, but because healing is not linear.

But this time, you'll notice it sooner. You'll catch the pattern as it's forming. You'll pause before the spiral. You'll come back faster. You'll anchor yourself in truth instead of shame. And you'll do it without shaming yourself into submission.

Because now, you know the truth:

You were never broken.

You were never too much.

You were never meant to live in survival.

You were always meant to rise. To lead with softness. To protect your peace. To build a life that feels like yours. To be trusted. Seen. Chosen by yourself first. This isn't about being "healed." It's about being honest and being present. Being **whole**, even in the messy middle. Even when the old patterns creep in. Even when you forget for a moment what you've worked so hard to remember.

As you close this book, I don't want you to create a new checklist or a 12-step plan for personal evolution. I want you to **listen**. To your body. To your breath. To the voice inside you that's been quietly waiting for permission to speak again. She's still there. And she's ready. Ready to rise. Ready to lead. Ready to reclaim the space she gave up to keep the peace. Ready to trust herself again. Ready to stop shrinking in rooms where she was born to expand. You don't have to become someone new. You just have to stop hiding the truth of who you already are. This is your invitation. Not to hustle harder. Not to prove your worth. Not to meet expectations that were never yours to begin with. But to live like a woman who remembers her power. Unapologetically. Unfiltered. Aligned, at last.

And if you're wondering what happens next?

You live it. You start showing up differently. You choose presence over performance. You notice what no longer fits and have the courage to let it go. You speak up when silence feels easier. You trust your yes. You honor your no. You make peace with imperfection. Not perfectly. But intentionally. From a place of grounded clarity, not reactive urgency. You let it be awkward. You let it be slow. You let it be messy. You let it be real. Because growth isn't always loud—it's often invisible. It's not in the before-and-after pictures. It's not in the highlight reels. It's in the quiet in-between. It's in the pause before overcommitting. The breath you take before rushing to say yes. The grace you give yourself when the old story tries to take over. It's in the moments no one else sees but you. It's in the choosing. Choosing yourself—again and again—without apology or permission. Choosing your peace even when no one claps for it. Choosing your voice even when it shakes. You're not behind. You're not broken. You're becoming. And every time you return to the truth of who you are, you rise a little higher. Every time you say, "This matters to me," you reclaim ground. Every time you rest without guilt, you rewrite history. Every time you say, "Not this time," to the old patterns, you build new ones. This is the beginning. Not of a hustle. Not of a brand. But of a life lived **on your terms**. A life led with intention. A life that honors your rhythm, not someone else's timeline. A life that gives as much space to softness as it does to strength. A life where you don't have to split yourself in two just to be accepted. You've done enough performing. You've carried enough weight. You've tried to fit into blueprints that were never meant for you. Now it's time to build something new. Rooted in alignment. Fueled by peace. Carved out by truth. Sustained by self-trust. Reinforced by values that feel like home. Let the rest fall away. Let the shame go. Let the guilt expire. Let the "shoulds," expectations, and masks fall off. **Let it burn.** Let it all make room for what's real. Let the life that's genuinely yours rise from the ashes. This is your becoming. This is your return. This is your rebirth. And you are already enough. Not because of what you've done, but because of who you are. Not because of what you've earned, but because of what you've chosen. And every time you choose yourself, you show the next woman that she can too. So walk forward—softly, boldly, honestly. And keep rising.

BURN THE BLUEPRINT

You're free now.

You're home.

You're her.

About the Author

Magan Avila is a speaker, writer, and mentor passionate about helping women break free from the expectations that keep them small. After years of chasing hustle culture, striving to meet invisible timelines, and wearing burnout like a badge of honor, she reached a breaking point that led her to redefine success.

Through her own journey of unraveling perfectionism and redefining what truly matters, Magan invites women to release unrealistic expectations and create lives that feel aligned, intentional, and authentic. Her voice is raw and relatable, blending personal stories with deep insights that speak to the heart of every woman who has ever felt behind, overwhelmed, or disconnected from herself. Magan's work is a reminder that healing is not linear, timelines are meant to be broken, and joy is not something to be earned — it's something to reclaim.

When she isn't writing or speaking, you'll find Magan soaking in the chaos and beauty of raising her two boys, growing in alignment alongside her husband, and creating space for the kind of conversations that remind women they are already enough — exactly as they are.

Magan loves connecting with women who are on their own journey of alignment and becoming. You can find her on Facebook at Magan Avila or join her on Instagram @multipreneurmagan for daily inspiration and real talk about life, business, and healing.

www.ingramcontent.com/pod-product-compliance
Lightning Source LLC
Chambersburg PA
CBHW070649050426
42451CB00008B/324